Back Roads

Back

Roads

poems

Patricia Henley

Carnegie Mellon University Press
Pittsburgh 1996

ACKNOWLEDGMENTS

I wish to thank Purdue University for support during the completion of this manuscript, and the editors of the following magazines and anthologies in which certain of the poems in this volume have previously appeared, some in slightly different form:

Carolina Quarterly, The Chowder Review, Cottonwood Review, De Humanities, The New Salt Creek Reader, Outerbridge, Three Rivers Poetry Journal, New Women Poets, Woman Poet, the West, and *Northwest Review.*

Several of the poems in the first and second sections of *Back Roads* were published originally in *Learning to Die,* Three Rivers Press, 1979.

The Publication of this book is supported by grants from the National Endowment for the Arts in Washington, D.C., a Federal agency, and by the Pennsylvania Council on the Arts.

Library of Congress Catalog Number 95-067964
ISBN 0-88748-217-1

Printed and bound in the United States of America

10 9 8 7 6 5 4 3 2 1

CONTENTS

in memory of Anne Sexton

I.
Learning to Die
(1972-1976)

FISHWOMAN

Pinched arrows of light target
the baby's eyes red and matted.
Flies with iridescent wings
graze there. She covers
the crib with cheesecloth,
lights a cigarette. The smell
of sour milk smears the bed,
the slanting porch. Her breasts
rest flat and stretched. Meaty
bullheads wait at the black river.
She'll crouch in a high wind,
her brown legs dry as ashes,
her hair a stiff oily helmet,
fingering the cane-pole,
waiting like the fish,
empty-eyed, with no tears.

IMMIGRANT

for Anna Swiezy, my Bohemian grandmother

She shored in Baltimore,
ten years old, reckoning
streets bricked in gold.
Instead, linoleum cabbage roses
flowered and smelled of urine
in every room
she ever lived in.
Days, she labored
candy factories and glass works.
Nights, she learned shorthand,
scheming to barter for indoor plumbing,
oranges, silk stockings.

At twenty-five she moved midwest
and married a game warden,
prompt in his brown uniform.
She wrote stories and answered
contest jingles. They always
voted Democrat. Early on
his heart deadlocked,
left her in her widow bed.
Palsy stung her feeble,
her mouth brooking saliva,
her legs slow. On the chiffarobe,
Christ was thorn-rimmed,
thin and dark, draped
in glass bead rosaries.
Mornings, she typed,
piling up manuscript like counterfeit,
the story of the new world,
toilets, factories, suffragettes.

FRIENDS

Thirteenth summer: the pump
stays primed, the well never runs dry.
Two girls find a twenty dollar bill
along a gravel road and spend
half of it on nail polish.
Five inning softball games stud the days.
Blackberries bleed and pear full
bending branches hide the chicken house.
Dark nights, television folds
dull gray aprons of light
around them, the popcorn bowl.
They sleep near the screened-in porch:
rooted in the feather bed,
their fingers oily with butter,
they fiercely rub between their thighs,
practicing, learning to take.
The moon chalks shadows on the peeling wall.

SECRETS

The house knows:
in every room she's wired
for a crisis. Once they mainlined
seamy stories all night
under the candle's glance,
bartering genitals.
Now the bed on claw feet
follows her around,
nagging. Sheets threaten,
the Indian bedspread
crumples, leering.
She smothers fantasy
membrane by membrane
back into her brain pan.
He pours the sauterne.
She boils water
for the saffron rice.
Passing her in the kitchen
he squeezes her breast
by habit.

MOTHER NURSING

Summer steamrolls over them.
Once a week friends gather,
glut the room with music.
The father plays electric bass.
She serves iced tea
of sassafras and anise root
then fades into her pumpkin shell,
using last year's poems
for paper towels.
Maternity smocks tent the body
stretched in two home births.
Shedding half her paisley blouse,
she nurses the infant
and chews soft fingernails,
remembering the mirror,
her housewife's thighs folding back
like broken bird wings,
the web of blood,
breasts kindled to the brim
and hot.

MOTHER AND SON

Empty ragged soup cans rim
the kitchen sink, the table.
Television's narcotic flicker
greases the room. She does
his arithmetic homework.

you are stupid like I was

before a laborer invented her,
trenching neat blood tunnels
front and rear, chapping her oily thighs
bruised, his beard, callouses, teeth, tattoo
stamping her flawed
with son.

He went on the road,
stayed on the road. She and the boy
soak in sleep. He grips her,
his small teeth grinding,
mirrors, eyes, bicycle wheels.

SPINSTER

She stored the old country
in a cedar box: folded quilts,
stiff, brown-tinted photographs of plump children
with a solemn wet-nurse. Her shrewd eyes
refused to shrink, to be female, shy.
Pride seamed her taffeta,
held the table's oilcloth straight,
nurtured African violets ledging
dining room windows. At twenty-two
she denied her only suitor and said
she didn't like the way he walked.
No man unlocked her camisole.
She did for others: stretching
washed crocheted curtains
on pine frames in the drying sun,
pinching creamy yeast dough
into braids and buns. Afternoons,
her hearing aid turned down,
she rocked before TV, her rosary
pooled between her knees.

SURVIVORS

He locks them in and goes to work,
burying them away from other men
without even grave clothes. The woman
is large for the narrow walls,
awkward in goose flesh. The girl
sits in the empty tub rocking
and rocking. After the first hour
they cape their bare shoulders
in bleached out towels
and begin the nursery rhymes.
They count the floor tiles,
the ceiling blocks. Porcelain
echoes every word. By four o'clock
they've battered themelves, loving
the hollow ring of bone against basin,
wearing the bruises like badges or power.
The cottage sprays silent beyond the keyhole:
egg grows gummy on the breakfast plates,
a sheet of sunlight shrinks on the floor.

RETURNING FROM THE FUNERAL

My brother and I drive east,
taking turns, not talking much,
just bad weather and bad food.
A mountain range lies ahead,
a pale blue bone. Clouds
scuttle away from us.
I am anxious to be there,
home, away from the aging,
the smothered talk
of what went before,
the stuff of old photo albums.
Until this funeral I never saw
your hands be still. But your lips
were drawn together, the pearl rosary
mounted precisely so.

I inherit a cardboard box
of documents and love letters,
proving you a passionate woman.
The man I call my lover quotes
the Tibetan Book of the Dead:
there should be no mourning
and there isn't, but would you say,
if you could, for all the wrong reasons.
I want to know I'm alive,
eating egg rolls and making love.
I imagine that, tinging your death
with my blood pealing like church bells,
leaving the flat land, the farmhouses,
all set in such staid symmetry.

HOUSE OF MANY FATHERS

For years I built a secure house
of dreams and paper, appointing
even brass beds and patchwork quilts.
In every room there was a father
amid desks and reading lamps.
Every father petted me to sleep.
My flesh was soft as butter
and just as sweet.

Neglected in his motel room,
my blood father telephones me
once a year at three AM.
We talk like old beery friends
but it's late for us.

The house of many fathers
is my prison, all double locks,
institutional food,
handcuffs and sex
with strangers.
Every morning after, I wake
the arsonist in me. Hair tangled
and tongue swollen, she determines to burn
but never finds the broken matches.

I'M STILL LEARNING

He writes
from an Indian reservation
in South Dakota where he lives
with Jesuits and is joyful,
but celibate.
I write back, me too,
though not by choice
and I wish
I could send you
a little in a letter.

The next day
in a first grade class
I recite *Little Orphan Annie*
all the while remembering
Baltimore, the time
we dropped acid
in the park
a warm day in January and he spent
an eternity explaining the leaf machine
to my son
then we left the park
crossing Charles Street
against the light
carrying the boy and his dumptruck
traffic blistering around us
I can't tell the cars coming
from the cars going and we double
over laughing and I shout
what is this madness and he says well
it isn't Santa Barbara
at the beach

Where have I been in two years?
I'm still learning
to roll a good joint and one of the sweeter sounds
is still my name
from the mouth of a new man.

GEMINI

It's party time.
In the yard, someone
is giving away squash
from the garden. Others
locked in the living room
lick the red from their eyes.
My mouth falls slack in the drink:
siamese twins come on like a team,
straight lady and sweet mama.
One settles into this life,
a stone in a streambed.
The other pastes paper wings
to shoulderblades, trying
to fly. Sky wads her throat
like black cotton, stars sliver there
like glass. Blame hovers her usual beat.
I pretend not to notice the smooth brome
deep and wet as a love bed.
It's always this way,
the two of us closing our eyes
in order to see. All my letters lie,
sins of omission.

CHOICES

I slept under a stone,
not knowing night, dreams.
Waking, I cover myself with losses.
My young son comes into the morning bed,
his limbs sleep-weak, and I am grateful
for this small distraction,
his breath like sour warm flowers
on my cheek. He kisses
my eyelids, both raw
from slipping tears into air
all day before, all day.

I want to read the future forked.
It can't be done. There are rooms to be swept.
I speak questions blankly
with disappearing ink oiling my mouth.
The rituals become the answers
become the rituals: lighting the evening fire,
washing the fruit.

LEARNING TO DIE

My son cries his loneliness to the wall:
already he is separate
from himself and wants
another creature,
mirror of milk and hands
to hold rags of fear
together through dawn.
All day he builds paradise
with scissors, paper, tape.
He forgives the night its threat.

I collect books on this subject.

Each time desire,
delicate as a fern's shadow,
pierces the wall of my womb,
each time I throw back
the bedsheet and fuck,
death is there like a voyeur,
dressed like a whore and painted,
too rich to touch.

I want to bring her to the kitchen,
change her name. Give her sky
to drink from a cup and scar
my heart with her eyes.

II.
Building Site
(1977-1980)

MEDITATIONS OF A WOMAN SLOWING DOWN

1.

The potter stacks the kiln,
pot to brick. From earth
he shapes cups, carved
with lions mating,
to hold earth: yarrow
that grows like a white lace fire
waiting to be struck tea
in some yogi's belly.

2.

The house, square as a book
and hard as a man, collects dust:
the road comes into the house
with a life of its own,
powdering rugs and bedclothes.
But outdoors: the sky becomes large,
canyon walls are mother round
where wind fringes lupine.
I make my request of the stones:
teach me to die
cradled, crushing camomile
on the path, as evening comes,
slow as malt syrup, clouds knifing sky.

3.

The treasure of their space opens:
she is brown and stands on the porch
building a wind chime
of rusty nails and thread.
He lies in the hammock.

The sun screams *july, july.*
This is what we are about:
the rhubarb pie, the talk
of past loves, admitting that
at one time or another
we each lie awake
counting the same question marks
like sheep.

4.

The grinder is still.
In the bowl, sun saddles new rice flour.
On the table,
an orange poppy
silks open like a woman.

BETWEEN SYLLABLES

Some men are more mad than others:
the skull and cross-boned bottle near the iron pump,
wind boiling in the trees and cries
are a language forgotten in the crib.
Her dress sash trails the floor.
Her eyes are those of a small mute animal
focusing on red, strawberries
on the table, grandfather's suspenders
as he claims her skin, lye-burning
her legs, his flat goat eyes dead.

Her lover will braille scars each night.
The old man will be more real
than most grandfathers, more real
than a brown photograph torn
from the rotogravure,
photograph of a man in uniform
with a thin smile as flat as his eyes.
Strawberries on flowered oilcloth
will always choke her brain with noise.
Like the rest of us, she will weep
from the same eyes all her life.

My body is a temple of the Holy Spirit.

Our bodies: Jews who laugh in their grief,
kicking and burning the corpses of Arabs,
terrorists who kill with demon teeth
in their hearts, tasting death mud
in their own mouths, children in pajamas
who know blood raining on the roof
in their sleep, children who nightmare

the blood of their dead fathers
leaking from televisions: our bodies.

A man tattoos his forearm with the first name
of his first love. That faded blue script
will be the same at forty as it was at fourteen,
but the women he has loved
will rise up and join hands, links of stars
like tears in his eyes, warp of shadow
in his gray beard.

There is no escaping
the tremor lacing lost sleep,
the dawn light of eyes inviting hands,
the chanting and chanting on the lips of God
in each of us: between syllables
the silence contains the fire we've known,
god-fires to napalm. A full red moon
in the window mirrors the sun
to pagans and saints alike. An infant
lies on a bed of bones,
suckling of an old woman
drawing her last breath.

All of this occurs in the silence
between the pine cone
breaking from the branch and rattling
to the ground. Music
that has always been there
reaches into my ears:
we are the same skin.

HANDS

I've given up my hands.
They go their own way,
nicked and scratched, learning
the shape of tools,
a hammer's weight,
the way a saw shares plywood.
Once my hands sat back
in repose, fat cats,
not of much use. Now
my son brings me an orange
from the clay bowl. I reach
for my pocket knife
to peel it.

SLAUGHTERING THE GOAT

One shot and the killing is over,
quickly as trimming a thumbnail:
two narrow ropes of blood
shoot from his nostrils,
his head goes limp,
the eyes like amber marbles.
One friend slits the brown throat,
severs the neck and tosses the horned head aside
for young laying hens,
gone a little mad,
pecking red grass.
Flakes of blood fall
on black and white feathers.

I've hidden from this for years.
Menstrual blood. Finger cuts.
Random violence in films.
Death was a book left unread,
locked on the shelf.
Shadow like a dark cloth
moves over us
as we salvage the skin.
Pearly membrane between skin and flesh
gives easily under the knife
as if meant to be dissected.

Next winter our house will wear squall
in the rafters
like song in the hair,
crown of tears, dwarf mirror,
a child falling like fruit,
so new, with sky and clouds

in each pale eye.
I will catch the child and cut the cord.
Birth and death ride the same sure horse.

I hear music from a nearby cabin
where it is an ordinary day: jazz and whiskey.
I touch the neck and take some pleasure
in the blood on my hands.
I read birth in the stain.
The day grows late and cold
as the hard Arkansas stone
we sharpen knives on.

EVEN IN BLAZE

A small rain falls on lovers
lying in lambsquarter
caught in the bite
of the mother's moon tooth.
Tribal fire, tribal cries,
burn nearby. He
is thunderbolt, she,
a core source of light.
They come home, come home,
to grave, to cradle
under ribs of rotting timber
creaking in wind.
Even in blaze burning palms and cheeks
as they touch, ash exists,
cold and inevitable.
The salmon decays on his bones
even as he spawns upriver.
The picked lilac falls into dust.

DEAD HORSE

I think of dying every time we meet.
How we once made a suicide pact.
Our demise was certain, a script,
and rage ran like a crack
down the vessel, our love or need.
Now we never talk about the past.
It's all next week or next winter,
pass the wine and let me bum another cigarette.
At your kitchen table, shame
like a rash makes me itch
to be out that door.
Mistakes I've made bang against my brain
like a dirge, heartworm's lament,
until I know some small, live thing:
nightshade winding around
roots of a yellowing cottonwood,
roosters crowing in mist before sun up.
I never tell you how it feels
to carry a soiled heart
into a room full of blazing light,
running away.

INSTEAD, SPARKS

Among the Persian rugs and cushions,
the tea you offered,
the wine we drank, what happened there?

You tell me the kind of woman you are.
I know this about you:
you are the woman who trails a white lilac
at her side, walking steps behind a man
in a dream he may never share.
The pollen of a lifetime floats around you,
veil of honey, *what may be.*
I am watching from my kitchen window.
Coffee thickens in the pot.

We could have been more polite
or distant—stars in different galaxies—
Instead you lean so easily into my arms.
Let us brush one another's hair
until sparks fly!
Running home from you after midnight
I see the bright rhododendrons glow
under moonlamp like exotic fish
set free
in a dark leafy sea.

BUILDING SITE

for Karen Hamilton

It is shelter we speak of one Sunday afternoon,
walking by the pond, with the cattails rusting
in autumn chill, blackbirds nesting one hour before sunset.
We crawl under a barbed wire fence, admitting
we each once thought it possible
to love more than one man.

Three junipers, grandmothers robed in corded bark,
cast the clearing like a spell, *build here, settle.*
You point to the skeleton of willows, promise
of flower in spring, dream of porches,
gin and tonics, work at bay, summer sky: evening
sunlight only a gold band above Bryant Mountain.
Applewood, fir, walnut, oak,
                                        juniper smoke
fragrant from the chimney,
shale roof and snow drifting to the eaves,
O dream of drawknife, tongue and groove,
cross braces, stone
shelter. A place to pass the seasons.

For each of us there can be only one home,
heartsafe against night's cold, scab rock
and sage. Practice home. Build.
To break the ice in the stream: today's desire.
Bright green moss still grows there.

III.
Back Roads
(1991-1994)

WISHES FROM A MIDNIGHT WIND

for Michelle Byrne

Two girls giggle beneath the long window.
They cast their sweet girl
breath and hair and thighs here and there
toward whatever boy happens by. Tonight
it's the village soccer player
and though I do not understand his French
I know he brags. He thinks
this is the way to win them. His plan
to buy a car. A trip to Paris he took
when he was twelve. His brutal game.

Today your letter arrived: a traveler's event.
And even the stamp—some tractor from before the war—
makes me a little homesick. The roses
you've planted figure large; the trunk
from the flea market; the ticking
you need for its interior, the cheer.
A man has entered your crooked house
by the railroad tracks. He tells you that
he loves your garden-soiled knees and hands.

In this letter your surrender
catches light like a secret thread
put there by a cunning weaver.
Of course, I have wishes for you;
and I suspect those wishes might be
both more and less than wishes you will get
from wedding guests next summer.
Every day a few androgynous hours
of quiet. A dawny garden.
No madness, no insomnia.
The patience required to be a woman.
You don't need me to tell you,
Life is long and so many moments

you won't   want   to be   bothered.
But more and always: that your heart
not be the heart of a thief
when you steep yourself in time
to write a poem. Stingy or afraid.
Never that.

Here, in Provence,
midnight wind rolls and hurls
Cezanne's plane tree.
A kind man, love of my life—
I believe in such things—
retrieves my tar-stained dress
from the *gite's* clothesline.
The chapel glows blondly in the night.
The girls are green the way the orchard
pears are green.

WE WERE INTO THE RUM

for Stern

Did I ski that Christmas? Were there mountains?
What romance—the *West*—beckoned me
to Bozeman where only the most
ephemeral wafer of my being
danced in the hall, danced in the kitchen.
There was usually Lena Horne
or Linda Rondstadt or the Mills Brothers singing.
No one there knew you. How odd that seemed.

My heart moved in the shape of a map.
Deep in my real body, the one that seizes
whatever's next—no small gesture—
I remembered Chicago, brick interior walls,
a Gauguin show, your handhold, rushing
from painting to painting, whispering
his life, the life mattered
to us, the foolhardy courage of voyages
and young girls and selling his belongings.

It was cold. You bought me a bright blue hat
at a second hand store. In the Polish restaurant
the steam and clatter loved us. Those heavy mugs
loved us. And the regulars, the way they shouted.
I think they were shouting about football and the mayor.
For about five minutes we wanted to be regulars.
And the waitress, blond, pimpled, but cheerfully so—
she told me how long it took her to grow out

her bangs. How she almost gave up.
She encouraged me. We didn't have much money.
A twenty dollar bill. And you said, Let's pretend
it's the old days and see how far we get on this.

In my life I've seldom been in just one place.
In the mountains the streets are always calling.
This is not a blessing. Two trees,
their terrible limbs ash white, scratch the sky
over a man walking his sad black dog.
The woman with him stops and checks out the stars.

I remember your words you told me to remember,
a little light left. What racks, what restless history:
we brought every lover we ever had into our mutual night.
All those people of our embraces and goodbyes
swayed in that little light, chorus of veterans,
of outlaws. We were into the rum,
your fingers brushing your father's gravestone,
the grainy streets alive for just that day
within the fleeting lock of our arms.

STAR VIDEO

Step right up.
Come in, story seekers,
from the dark highway.
The hunger you have
is an old one. Check out
the salty dreams. Kisses.
Uncut. The hotheaded.
Vamps. Fools.
Laughter squeezed
from hurt and rage.
The worst heartbreaks
of childhood.
Betrayal.
Dead
ends.
In boxes black
and neat as Bibles.

Stroll the Couple's Sideshow.
You'll crave skin
telegraphs, the same
message to your brains.
Some nights this
is as close as you get
to negotiation
that matters.

Get in line. Go
ahead, take a mask.
Prophylactics for the psyche.
Winter's heart guards,
inside the lives of strangers,
their flat champagne.
With too much time
on your hands, you

might tell
too much truth.

How thick the veil.
How dull the day.
How flat the kiss.
How locked your hearts.

Next morning
you stir in bed and think
of clothes. Pink sweater.
Blue. Dream
of a big white shirt. Pleats
as crisp as new money.
French manicures. He hunts
for his socks. Outside,
sky rises like cream
in a jar. Too soon
to tell if it's a sunny day
or gray. You hear
the mean steps and curse
of one whose heart has turned
to ice or ragged teeth.
A regular on your street.

Some kind of rotting happens.
Trash accretes, midden pile
of the soul. Frame after frame.

The movies: our shabby
impulse toward religion,
toward what Stone Age
people know, gathered,
even now, in 1994, to watch
the birth of every mewling

infant born to them. They
pull themselves from leafy sleep.
Climb the hacked out steps
to caves where women kneel
and squat and bleed.

While you're there—
watching star videos,
away from windows,
denying windows—
winter roams again.
Better believe it.
Huge butcher.
Mucous gray,
ice gray, salt gray.
What you
could not imagine
in July. Road terror.
Huddling. The impatience
of woolens. A family
at the edge of town
taking turns
digging the dog's grave.

ABOVE THIS, OUTSIDE THIS

When you're angry you think
you'll live forever. War must
be like that: god of evil
teasing you with immortality.
You hear and see nothing
but the whir and dart of bullet-like birds
diving in a darkening copse,
heart-snarl as large as a house.
Nothing gets through.
Nothing has the chance to please you.
Not the stolid cows.
Or notes children have pencilled
in the bottom of a wooden box:
empty all gone.
Not an old aunt's kindness.
Or a flavor of ice cream
you once had in Nevada.
Not the blue fringe of a cowboy shirt
you wore when you were four.
Not a yellow shovel.
Not speed. Not the aerodynamic
curve of your car slicing
the pearly summer haze.
Not trees. Not taiko drummers
or an Irish lullaby.
Not touch. That wooden interruption.
Not the stare of a grasshopper
on the tree of heaven.
Not the cardinals picking over
thistle seeds. (Some part of you
above this, outside this, sees
their thatched red chests and thinks
coldly, *female.*) Not the jokey
voices of workers tearing
out a sidewalk. Or
the clean bite of gin

on the tip of your tongue.
Particularly not that.
You have to sight
your crippled self
at least one thousand times
before you know her.
To love her takes a lifetime.
Make way. She's big.

BACK ROADS

Sin is enslavement to what you don't know about yourself.
—John Sanford
The Kingdom Within

Cold beats about their ankles.
Two women push a piano
in snow, an upright, a little
out of tune, with
veneer missing from six
keys. Bertha's, a bar,
is just across the street,
the windows chunks of yellow
light. This is memory.
From Baltimore. A rusted iron gate,
an orange snow fence
barely glimpsed through the woods,
there's always something
obstructing my sight. I can't
call it vision. Yet.

Simple information only
you can know is hard
to come by. Sometimes
upon waking I can't tell
the sound of the insects
from the sound of the birds.
I start all over from scratch.
I'm not sure what matters.
Hills rise up beyond
the river and I count
the high water signs.
In Delphi, poor town
of second hand shops,
there is a little brass girl
with her palm out
offering water from a fountain.

On a sunny day
I think, This, this is what
matters.

Sin. A word we skid away from.
Too much Catholic school
in that word.
It glittered once, didn't it?
Once upon a time
we thought we were very bad, but those
were just experiments.
We sinned the way a baby explores
his own shit. Even now maybe God
perceives us that way.
I think of Matisse when I'm sad,
the way those priestly vestments
nearly leap from the walls of his villa
in Nice, the crescent moons on his cross.
When is the love of paradox and joy
a sin? When is gossip? Waste?
Sorrow? Giving? Aversion?
I tried to make a sun map
of the yard. I couldn't sit still.
A turtle came into the fern bed
and stayed two days. He has mastered
becoming leaf. Moles persist,
their fur as dark and thick
as clouds of a storm you can't ignore.
Likewise, the footfalls on the deck,
a pantry full of food, sex,
basketball, wildflowers
like a cottony bundle of old quilts.

Who is it who tells me what to do?
Get down that road. I know it's dark.
Sit still until like magic—

though you can't call it magic—you see
to the bottom of the murky river.
One lane bridge,
slow traffic, moonlight
slipping across the shiny railroad tracks.
Just watch
yourself jog, cut back,
detour.

WHAT WE LEARN TOO LATE

You invent nothing.
It's all there. Given.
Gifts. Bliss. The dance
of him leaning over you
at the party. Backed
to a wall you whisper, *Come closer.*
Out on the deck
two barefoot women sing
acapella across a beer keg.
Famous people have long departed.
You stroll and kiss around
the village alleys in the dark
and leaf and cork of spring.
You in your harem pants,
he in paisley suspenders,
his white shirt pearly,
bloused beautifully in the moonlight,
his hand on your silk waist—
there is no other word
for what he does but *possession.*
Dreams of your old souls
sing out romance like an old radio.
Can you imagine palm trees,
art deco, somewhere? You've
done it now: entered the riches
of a district from which
there is no retreat, save
through the blind heart's breaking
and breaking.

MINING FOR CLARITY

November. Sounds like something used
to smother. You teach me
chess down under
in a coffee bar lit by
young, ambitious faces.
I have trouble thinking
that way. Late. At night.

When I tell you
to slow down and burrow
into yourself, it's me
I'm scolding. Tiresome arguments
like luggage I've lost the keys to
and carry from one bright and migrant home
to the next.

Sometimes I wonder what
your own locked struggle will be
in five years or ten.
And will I be there pitching
rocks across the ditch of terror
to help you with a wall
or will I hear about you
second-hand, a scrawled note on
a mutual friend's postcard from Chinatown
or Paris?

Mining: it is a little like
going into mountains. But there
you have a map.

Come, braided fig. Come, cherrywood.
Scent of ginger, lime pickle.
All the small appeasements.
And yet—

the used car lot across the street
is nearly always empty. Not quite a car
graveyard.

I think I want
to move. I think I want
my old life back,
the old laundry basket,
one handle torn, the ochre peaks
of houses near downtown,
that gloom reminding me of D.
H. Lawrence, bloom of androgeny. A job
in a little brick library.
I can imagine it.

A day takes so much boring care.
The wrinkle of a sock against your sole.
How hard to hold to gratitude.

THE JAZZ, THE SLEEP, THE SORROW

When you wake up from a nightmare
what color would you call the light
at five in the morning, blue-vein
through the rice paper blind?
You say you've had a nightmare?
Coming at something like a trot
through your sleep—not a terror,
not a gallop, but still, kicking up
the garden, all those seedlings crushed
beneath indifferent hooves. You find
out, don't you, what's really on your mind.
Light like a blue vein under the tattoo
we call a day of time, tattoo
on the hide of God. The basket where
you keep the linens, the lid askew
like a Mexican hat, the horses
blue and brave as cave drawings
on the spread—cheerful mess.
You have heard rumor of this
all your life. Holy books
are full of it. Songs and gossip.
Fairy tales. Your mother's
warnings. You had maps. Not
the most accurate, but you became
a good navigator, dragging a clumsy satchel
of trial and error, trial and error.
Trial and error. And now
you have come into the place
of your beloved and he into yours.
Adjacent gardens you might call them,
seeming infinite—you can fool
yourself into that—and fat
with weeds and flowers and thorns and

more than rumor ever
led you to believe. Sorrowful jazz.
Mysterious wool of sleeping close.
You did not know that choosing
someone to love would mean desiring
and fearing death
in the arms of that someone.
You did not know how—once you
entered the charm of the garden,
once you pulled apart the puzzle
of the wall—the nightlocks
would seize shut and broken behind you,
shut and broken behind you

ON ROATÁN

Sometimes after the last boat
we dilly-dally in the sunny lane
waiting for the lime pie girl.

Her mother's lardy crust melts
in your mouth. A trail
of seed beads unravels

across her bodice. Rain
when it comes
is dense, pewter-like

and we find out just how solid
an island is and sweet,
so sweet

we're almost bored,
our minds beach empty
for a change. If we have a curfew

we pretend we don't know about it.
Blue and red bedsheets lift
us up and I hear

the way a baby hears:
knock of grackle feet on the roof,
gritty hum of a wheelbarrow in gravel.

Buttery whir of the fan.
Honey nap. Honey sand.
Honey moon. Honey rain.

Always there comes a time
to rub the lamp of desire
down to the tarnish where

the laws of mystery are inscribed.
The lime pie girl's satin dress
is the color of camomile.

She hoots beside the bamboo,
Hot pie. Five lempira.
No more tomorrow.

DAUGHTER

Our daughter. The one we dream.
The one we brave. She'll say,

My father taught me all you
ought to expect
of love, the insistence
of it, heart exposed
to lenient heart.

Until she met my father
my mother cleared
the field of her heart
of stones—words—over and over.
She liked the rough fit of her
palm against the stones,
the cadent exercise. She worked
too much and sometimes she looked
startled up at us. It seemed
she did not know us then.
But we knew her and wanted
all the silly things she carried
in her pockets, her play voices.
Love has the force

of moving water, my father always said,
to flood, to carve, to change.
His drum was blue. It was a singing drum.
Their conversation curlicued,
in ornament, in word play.
They liked steamy movies, corny songs.
My mother was older than my father.
We were an odd and merry family.
They said they found me
in a patch of babies.
They said they knew me by my kindred eyes.
We hugged in bookstores

or at the kitchen sink or by the back door
in seven shades of sunset.
A trail slanting to the ocean
was a proper place to hug or dance.
Bright azaleas would be bursting,
seals would be barking. They said
the Eskimos called making love
making laughter. My father kept watch,
my mother taught me to skip
and talk nonsense. We were
always astonished by our existence,
the brief alignment of our bodies on the planet,
wild felicitous improv.